Better Communication

By

Richard A. Mulvey

By the same author:
Books / CD's / Training DVD's

1. The Will to Win
2. Time Management
3. You've only got 4 minutes
4. Handling Objections, Closing the Sale
5. Better Communication
6. Stress Management
7. Negotiate a Better Deal
8. Managing Meetings
9. Body Language
10. Getting New Customers...Keeping them for ever
11. Selling Quality... at your Higher Price
12. Delivering Exceptional Customer Service
13. Selling The Dream
14. Selling over the Telephone
15. Presenting For Profit
16. Selling Face to Face
17. Change Management
18. Memory Management
19. Achieving Peak Performance
20. Decisions

Published by: **Perception Business Skills**

ISBN 1 - 919951 - 77 - 6

First edition 1998
Second edition 2000
Third edition 2004

Book Design and Layout by Perception
Cover Design by Richard Mulvey

Published by:

Perception

P O Box 201622
4016 Durban North
South Africa
Phone +27 31 5635316 Fax: +27 31 5635432
e-mail: info@richardmulvey.com
website: www.richardmulvey.com

Contents

Introduction

In this book, you will learn a range of communication techniques that will help you earn more money, give you greater prestige and pleasure and increase your power in the work place.

A bold statement? We shall see.

It's not what you know, it's how you communicate what you know, that really matters.

Throughout this book, we will cover a wide range of communication techniques for use in:

One to One Communication
One to Many Communication
Writing Letters, Reports and Advertisements
Getting your Powerful Message Across
Communication to Influence and Persuade
Communication to Motivate
Communication with the Opposite Sex

This is not a book about using correct English or any other language. Accuracy is important but getting the message across is more important. Language is a tool that we use to communicate but the tool should never become more important than the task.

What is communication?

Right from the outset, it is important that we agree exactly what is being discussed here. So, what is communication?

Well, it can be a lot of things of course, but for this book "Communication is the process of imparting information or emotion in a way that is fully understood and hopefully accepted by the audience" (The person or people who are on the receiving end of the communication).

"Ah!" I hear you say. "Surely communication is a two way process? Isn't listening as important, or in fact more important, than talking? Isn't the process of communication the understanding of each other's point of view?"

"True" I reply "But........"

The responsibility for the success of any communication rests with the communicator, not the audience. This is an extremely important point and no progress will be made, until it is fully understood. It is the communicator, the person who initiates the communication, who must take responsibility to ensure that the message is fully understood by the receiver of the communication. Part of this process is listening to the point of view of the audience, to ensure that the communication is constructed in such a way as it will be fully understood (we will cover this in detail later). This does not change the fact that responsibility lies fully in the hands of the communicator.

So, for the purposes of this book, and to make my communication as simple as possible, (see rule 5) we will consider communication as a one way process, at least as a starting point.

General Rules

There are some general rules that should be explored in all communication. These rules apply equally to speaking as to writing. They apply to writing a book, a memo, an e-mail or an advertisement, speaking to a large audience or chatting to a friend in the pub. By using these rules in your communication, you will dramatically increase your ability to influence and persuade.

Rule 1 The responsibility for the success of any communication rests with the communicator.

Rule 2 The focus of any communication should be on the audience.

Rule 3 In advance of any communication, you should have a clear idea of your objective and your approach.

Rule 4 Good communications should be constructed with a beginning, middle and an end.

Rule 5 Keep it short and simple. The shorter the communication the greater the chance of full understanding.

Rule 6 Use Emotion. Buying decisions are often made emotionally. You will increase the chances of the audience buying your ideas if you tap in to their emotions.

Rule 7 Tell a story / paint pictures. People remember a story easier than facts and figures.

Rule 8 Listen.

Rule 1

The responsibility for the success of any communication rests with the communicator

We have already started to cover this rule in the introduction and that is not surprising. This rule is fundamental to all communication but it so often broken.

For instance:
I recently placed an advertisement on the wall of my local shopping centre. Our maid was looking for additional work and I offered to help. The main body of the advertisement looked like this:

Excellent Maid Available
Good with kids
Trustworthy
Hard Working
Can Cook
Available now
For more details.... etc.

Not my best bit of copy writing, but it worked.

In two days, I received 15 phone calls. 14 of the calls, however, came from people who were looking for domestic work. When I told Sheila (my wife) she said, “That’s stupid. Can’t they read?”

I was agreeing with her, of course, (well, she is my wife after all) and most of us would say, or at least think something similar. However, I was breaking the first rule of communication. The responsibility of this communication lies with me, as the communicator. If the communication has failed, it was my fault and it was necessary for me to rephrase the communication, to get the desired result.

I was in a friend’s office a few weeks ago. One of his team came in with a memo that he didn’t understand. My friend was abrupt and said, “Can’t you read English?” (How many of us have said something similar?) As the communicator, my friend was responsible for constructing the memo in such a way that the target audience would read and understand it, without a problem. In this of course, he failed and he should have been angry with himself, not his team member.

When communication breaks down in the office and a strike is looming, how often will you hear this lament from all sides “The trouble is, they never listen!”

Still though, the responsibility lies with the communicator. It is his or her responsibility to listen to the communicatee, in order that he or she can construct the communication in a way that will be fully understood.

Rule 2

The focus of any communication should be on the audience

This rule is obvious but so often broken.

In order to increase your chances of having your communication understood and accepted by the audience, it is essential that you construct it around their needs, not yours. There is no point is using long, complicated words in a children's book. They simply would not understand it.

In advance of any communication you should consider the needs of your audience. Then focus the thrust of your communication around those needs.

For instance:

Imagine you have made an appointment with your boss to discuss an increase in your salary. (Look, I know you are paid far too much already and you cannot imagine wanting more but just work with me here.) There are many different approaches that you may take, but consider the following and choose the one you feel to be the most appropriate.

I deserve more money because:

1. My wife's just had a new baby.
2. I'm a really nice guy.

3. Rehiring and training a replacement would be more expensive than a reasonable increase.
4. I have performed well this year.

Which one of the above is most likely to get you a salary increase?

In my seminars, number 4 is always the most popular choice but number 3 is the best answer.

You are already paid to perform well and your boss is most likely to worry about having to replace you if, he doesn't give you a reasonable increase.

Numbers 1, 2 & 4 focus exclusively on your needs. Number 3, on the other hand, focuses on the needs of your boss and is therefore much more likely to succeed.

Let's have a look at another example:

A car salesman was asked to present the new model to an audience of twenty people, on Sunday. Without enquiring about the audience, he constructed his speech around the things that he liked about the new car: fast, great on the corners, bucket seats, perfect for attracting the local girls, etc...

When he arrived for the presentation, he discovered that the audience was made up of 20 pensioners. Of course, he blew it!

Had he investigated who would be attending, he could easily have changed his presentation to include other features of the same car: reliable, economical, safe, etc....

In this way, he has a much better chance of securing the support of the audience.

The written word is just the same. An article in "Farmer's Weekly" about the state of our education system for instance, would be very different to an article on the same subject, in "Woman's Value". The opinions in the article may well be the same but they would be expressed in a way that would appeal to the different audiences.

When writing a monthly report on the performance of your department, there is a temptation to include what you consider to be important. This temptation (like many others) should be avoided. Prior to starting your report, ask yourself what the boss is interested in and construct your report around that.

For many years as a marketing man, I reported to a CEO who was an accountant. At the beginning, the relationship was poor because, in my arrogance, I communicated to him in the way I would like to have been communicated to. My reports were glossy and very descriptive. I used a similar style as I would with advertising. Unfortunately, they were wasted on the CEO. Eventually, I realised my mistake and my communication became short and to the point. My reports started with a financial overview and our relationship improved considerably.

When chatting to your colleagues in the bar after work, the conversation usually focuses on the interests of the speaker. Inevitably, if the conversation is to continue, it will deteriorate to the lowest common denominator of the group. This means that most group discussions in the bar after work are about work, money, sport, sex or telling jokes and possibly all of the above. (Have you heard the one about the secretary who asked for a pay rise when his boss was on her way to play golf .... perhaps another time?)

Next time you find yourself in a similar position, take one person aside and ask the question, “What do you like to talk about?” You will be amazed with the results. You will probably uncover saxophone players, amateur cycad growers and many other things you have never heard of. The more you know about people, the better able you are to communicate with them.

Professional communicators have this technique of focusing the communication on the needs of the audience, down to a fine art. I was listening on the radio to Bill Clinton some time ago, talking about some war or other. In quite a short speech, Clinton used the following phrase:

“I have to do these things for the sake of the World’s children”

Until that point in the speech, I was only half listening but suddenly I was fully attentive and hanging on his every word. I won’t go into the rights or wrongs of the battle, but the communication technique was brilliant.

Rule 3

In advance of any communication you should have a clear idea of your objective and your approach.

This raises two issues and we will deal with them separately.

The Objective

The objective of any communication is where you want to be at the end. The destination if you like. What you want to achieve.

Having an objective is essential. Starting to communicate without it is the same as going on a journey without a destination. The objective becomes the focus and controls your approach.

There are as many objectives as there are communications.

They could include:

To motivate your team
To increase your salary
To inform about a recent event
To raise funds for a charity
To find a job for your maid
To negotiate a better deal for your members
To persuade your partner to paint the house green.

Knowing your objective is an essential part of getting your message across, in a way that will be understood and accepted by the audience.

Problems start to appear when the objective is unclear, or when you try to communicate using multiple or mixed objectives. Every salesman will know that you can't sell two things at once and this rule applies to communication at all levels.

Examples of unclear or multiple objectives are as follows:

To increase your salary and get a better office
(Multiple Objective)

To negotiate a better deal for your members or if that fails, to make sure that their jobs are secure.
(Mixed Objective)

To persuade your partner to paint the house green or red or, at least, to smarten it up or something.
(Unclear Objective)

When your objective is not direct and specific, your approach becomes vague. You then dramatically reduce your chances of having your communication accepted.

The best way to ensure that you have a clear objective is to write it down. Get it into one sentence of 10 to 15 words. Avoid the use of the word "and" in your sentence as this will often appear when you have unclear or multiple objectives.

There was a famous American theatrical producer named David Belasco. He was, apparently, a difficult man who is remembered for many things, including this quote:

> "If you can't write your idea on the back of your business card, you don't have a clear idea."

This is a good discipline to try before you write your next report or presentation.

Once you have your objective, write it on the top of the piece of paper, and then plan your approach.

The Approach

If the object is your destination, your approach is the route.

Once you have your objective, you must consider what you know about the audience (Rule 2). The right approach will be the one that is most likely to convince your audience to accept your objective.

For instance:

Objective:	To motivate your team
Approach:	Offer financial incentives
Objective:	To increase your salary

Approach:	Prove your value to the company
Objective:	To negotiate a better deal for your members
Approach:	Demonstrate how the company would fail to manage without your members' support
Objective:	To persuade your partner to paint the house green.
Approach:	Threaten to withhold favours until agreement is reached.

I am not, of course, saying that I agree with the above approaches. Only you will know what is appropriate at the time and that will depend heavily on the needs of the audience.

Rule 4

All good communication has a Beginning, a Middle and an End

Whatever medium you choose for your communication, be it verbal, written, visual, or conceivably a mixture of the three, to get the best results and ensure that the communication is understood, it should be constructed with a beginning, middle and an end.

The Beginning

In the beginning, you get their attention and introduce the subject matter.

The start of any communication is vital. The person listening or reading must have their attention grabbed in the first few seconds or their mind will drift off, onto other things. They may seem as though they are paying attention but you will not have their full concentration. It will then be much more difficult to complete a convincing communication.

The beginning is known by many different names.

Newspapers call this the "Headline".

"Insurance Rep falls 20 stories into a swimming pool and survives"

Newspaper headlines are a very important part of the newspaper. We will skim the headlines until something interesting grabs us and only then, read the article. Headline writing is an important skill, because headlines sell newspapers.

Salesman will call it a "Hook" or a "Grabber"
."**Earn R5000 per month in your spare time"**

As old as time itself, this hook is still as effective as ever.

Authors would call it a "Title"

"How to win friends and influence people"

Or… "The one minute manager"

or even… "Who moved my cheese?"

All brilliant titles, vastly improving the chances of the books being taken from the shelf to the sales counter. I doubt whether "A good way to communicate with people" or "A better management style" would have had the same impact on the world.

Speakers would call it the “Introduction”

“Do you want to be rich? This afternoon we are going to talk about 10 ways to win at the casino”

Regrettably I missed this one.

Each of the above ‘beginnings’, creates an impact that gets attention and introduces the subject matter. The communication will be much less powerful if it is omitted.

Even when talking one to one, it is important to have a “Beginning” in your communication, if you want it to succeed. Don’t just launch into the conversation with the points you want to raise, start with a “Hook” or “Headline”.

For instance:

You’ve been trying to see your boss, John, for a week or so and eventually, you catch him in the corridor. You know you’ve only got a few seconds before he rushes off in an other direction, so you say.

“John, I’ve noticed our costs have shot through the roof recently. I’ve a couple of ideas that will help reduce costs, if you have a minute.”

That should grab his attention, don’t you think?

So, the beginning of your communication should grab the attention of the audience. It should also introduce the subject in a way that will have the audience looking forward to reading or listening to the communication. In many cases, this is achieved with your attention grabber. In others, you will have to outline what the audience is about to read or hear before proceeding.

In the “Speakers” example above, the first sentence, “Do you want to be rich?” is the "hook" that grabs the attention. The second sentence, “This afternoon we are going to talk about 10 ways to win at the casino”, is the "introduction" that has the audience on the edge of their seats.

The Middle

The middle section of your communication contains the main points you wish to raise. When compiling the middle section, consider the following:

1. Make sure that you only include items that will be of interest to the audience. You are not likely to be communicating to prove how clever you are, or how much you know. You are communicating to convince the audience and this will only be done if the content focuses exclusively on them.

2. Keep the middle section as short as possible.

3. Don’t try to include too many different items. The salesman will know that you can’t sell two things at once, so if your communication is trying to get agreement for something, stay focused and don’t get distracted.

During your communication, you will notice that your audience will not have the same level of attention throughout. Whether they are reading what you have to say, or listening to you, their attention will be good at the beginning, drift away a little and then pick up at the end. I would like to demonstrate this to you but you will have to follow the instructions exactly, to make sure the demonstration works.

Find a pencil and paper. (If you are reading this on a plane and you don't want to disturb the cabin staff, you can do this in your head, if you like).

When you are ready, I am going to ask you to turn to a page in this book and read the words at the bottom of the page once. Don't specifically try to remember them, read them at normal speed. Then close the book and write down all the words you can.

Okay? Turn to the bottom of page fifty three.

Which words did you remember? If you are a normal person and you didn't try to memorise them, just read them, you will probably have remembered the first three and the last one. That's the way it works with your communication. Your audience will remember the first part of the communication and the last, but not necessarily the middle. When you construct the middle section of your communication, you should have your most important point at the beginning and your second most important point at the end. This will be the best way to ensure that your audience remembers the key issues you are communicating.

The End

The beginning and the end are the most important parts of any communication but they are also the parts that are most often omitted. All too often, I hear people just stop talking, or read an article that ends abruptly, with the last point that was raised without a proper close. This leaves the audience hanging, uncertain of what happens next.

The end is essential, if the communication is to complete it's job. In the end, you need to accomplish two things:

1. Summarise the points raised, and

2. Get commitment from the audience

Shorter communication, of a paragraph or two, should not need a summary. If it is longer, summarise the points you raised, to remind the audience what has been discussed. If the communication is longer than a few minutes, the audience will have forgotten the earlier points and will need to be reminded prior to asking for agreement.

The final part is the close. The close tells the audience to make up its mind because no more points will be raised. The close will often call for some action on behalf of the audience, to indicate that they have accepted the thrust of the communication.

The method of communication by using a beginning middle and an end is common to many different communicators.

Salespeople know that you have to repeat things three times, if you want them to be remembered.

Tell them what you're going to tell them.
Tell them.
Tell them what you told them.

In other words,

The Beginning - Introduce your subject.
(Tell them what you're going to tell them)

The Middle - The main points.
(Tell them)

The End - Summarise and close.
(Tell them what you told them)

Advertisers use a different acronym, **AIDA**

Attention	The Beginning
Interest	Also The Beginning
Desire	The Middle
Action	The End

When constructing any communication, try to follow these three logical steps. You are far more likely to have your communication understood and accepted.

Rule 5

K.I.S.S.
Keep it Short and Simple

Short

If you can get your message across in 10 minutes, don't use 20. If the message can be squeezed into 5 Minutes, don't use 10. Even 5 minutes is too long for most messages, and a minute or even 30 seconds can easily be enough.

Why? The average human concentration span is very short.

Try this test:

From wherever you are sitting, find an inanimate object on which to focus your attention. It might be a chair, or a door, or even a glass of water, it doesn't matter. Now, try to focus your full attention on that thing for thirty seconds. ....

It's hard isn't it? After about ten seconds, your mind will begin to wander, then you pull it back, but 30 seconds is a long time to focus your attention on one thing.

Most communication gets to you at between 160 and 260 words per minute. Speakers speak and readers read at about that speed, so that is the speed that you receive communication. You think, however, at about 600 words a minute or more, so soon after you start to listen, your mind goes off in any number of different directions using the extra 440 words per minute.

Good communicators use their skill to keep your attention by constantly bringing new factors to think about, changing their speed, style or tone, using pictures to fill your mind or focusing on things that you like.

The shorter the communication, the easier it is to keep your attention and therefore, be convinced.

The electronic media, radio and television, discovered this early on in their history and they developed what is known as a “Sound Bite”.

A “Sound Bite” is a 10 to 30 second news item or article that stands on its own or is patched with other “Sound Bites”, into a story. Next time you watch an actuality program on the television, you will notice that most stories are broken into these 10 - 30 second chunks. The producers know this is about the length of time they have before they lose your attention.

Simple

You are not communicating to impress, (well probably not) you are communicating to get acceptance and understanding. By keeping your communication simple, you are more likely to achieve those ends.

Avoid using big words or too many words

I am sure that we have all come across examples of using 10 words where one would do. Politicians all over the World have been perfecting this form of communication for years.

"It has to be said, at this moment in time, that I will, under no circumstances, be able to make any meaningful contribution to the ongoing discussion without due consideration of the impact my disclosure may, or may not have on the voting public."

In other words, **"No Comment"**
A good rule to apply to your communication is :

"The 3 - 20 - 3 Rule"

When constructing any communication, try to avoid words with more than three syllables, sentences with more than 20 words and paragraphs with more than 3 sentences.

Try not to mix your metaphors. (You may let the cat out of the bag but you don't want to put it in amongst the pigeons, at the same time).

As has already been expressed at the beginning of this book, the ultimate purpose of the communication is to ensure that the message of the communicator is understood and accepted, not to impress the audience with the extent of the communicator's vocabulary. It is therefore, wise to avoid embellishment and reduce the communication to its shortest possible length.

Or, in other words, "Keep it short and simple".

Rule 6

Use Emotion.

Buying decisions are often made emotionally. When you look at that new car and feel that you would like to buy it (given the funds), what is creating that feeling in you?

Sure, the economy of the car and the large boot is nudging the practical side of the buying process but those things fade against its design, speed, colour, and status. All of which provide emotional reasons for the purchase.

In most cases, emotions control practicalities and our hearts rule our heads. If you can tap into those emotions with your communication, while you are explaining the practicalities, this will greatly increase your success rate.

Earlier in this book, I quoted President Clinton, "**I have to do these things for the sake of the World's children".** By making this emotional link, Clinton increases his chances of getting agreement from the audience.

Take a critical look at magazine and television advertising. You will see emotional triggers in almost every advertisement. Love, hate, desire, admiration, trust, longing, envy, sadness, joy, ... they are all there and they are all designed to influence our buying decisions.

But this does not just apply to advertising. Touching the emotions in all communication will greatly improve the success rate. Even a business communication, as formal as a letter from a representative to the factory manager, can include emotion.

The following paragraph appeared at the end of a letter, written by a very clever staff representative, to the Factory Manager.

"By securing the salary increases and settling the dispute you will gain the trust and respect of the whole factory and the admiration of the Management Board."

Which factory manager would not like the "trust and respect" of the people who report to him? Which factory manager would not like "the admiration" of his bosses? By the way, it worked!

Speakers the world over, have used emotion to gain support. The following two paragraphs say the same things. Which do you think will get the most support?

"We must all fight against crime. Please stand up, if I have your support." or

"There comes a time in every man's life when he has to stand up and be counted and for us, this is the time. We have stood by and blamed others while our friends and neighbours are robbed and brutally murdered, while our children are being raped on the streets and while our families are being forced to live behind bars to secure a measure of safety. Enough is enough! Now is the time to stand together, to rid ourselves of this nightmare. Who amongst you will not stand up and come

amongst you will not stand up and come with me, now, side by side? Together, we represent a powerful force for good. And when they ask us, we will tell them. We will not be beaten! We will not be beaten!!"

Okay, you can sit down again now, but I know you get the message.

Rule 7

Tell a Story

Stories are an important part of all human development.

From an early age, we are told stories. From those stories, we learn the difference between right and wrong, how society works and what happens if we don't eat our vegetables.

Every civilisation for the past 20 thousand years, have used stories to communicate important messages and we are used to getting information in this way.

When we are told a good story, we paint pictures in our mind that develop alongside the story. Our minds are much better equipped to remember pictures, so communications that include stories or pictures, will be remembered far longer than those that don't.

I have used the following quote before but it is such a good piece of communication, its worth repeating.

Winston Churchill could have said:
"The battle will be hard but we will carry on until we win."

But what he actually said was:

We shall not flag or fail
We shall go on until the end
We shall fight in France
We shall fight on the seas and on the oceans
We shall fight with growing confidence and growing strength in the air
We shall defend our island whatever the cost may be
We shall fight on the beaches
We shall fight on the landing grounds
We shall fight in the fields and in the streets
We shall fight in the hills
We shall never surrender

Rule 8
Listen

The above rules, from one to seven, were all to do with one way communication. However, as we have already discussed, your ability to listen is one of your most important skills as a good communicator. We are not good listeners but if we don't listen, and demonstrate that we have listened, we will not be good communicators either.

Why is listening difficult?

1. **Speakers get short term rewards**

From childhood, we learnt that making noises would get some action. As babies, we cried to be fed and at school, if we gave the answer we would be rewarded. Even at work, the talkers get the short term rewards and that encourages us to talk.

2. **We think we know more**.

When we are listening, we tend to make up our minds very quickly and believe we know more about what is being discussed than the talker, so we stop listening and just wait for an opportunity to talk.

3. **We think faster than we listen**

We discussed this earlier but as we listen to someone talking, we tend to think about other things as well which leads the talker to think that we are not listening at all.

Good listening takes a few skills and some practise. I have listed a few of the skills involved; the rest is up to you.

How to listen.

1. **Listen Actively**

Men are not very good at this technique but ladies have been doing it for centuries. When a lady is listening, she will tend to prompt the speaker to keep going by saying things like "No.... Really?" or "Go on.. tell me more." Men are not good at this at all but we can all learn to encourage the speaker.

2. **Check for understanding**

One good way to let the speaker know that you have been listening is to repeat back to them in your own words, what has been said. You may say something like "Let me get this straight, is what you have been saying this...?"

In this example, the speaker may say "No, not exactly that, more like this..."

3. **Be objective**

This is a useful habit to get into when listening. Try to suspend judgement until the speaker has finished talking.

4. **Empathise**

We often only see things from within our own frame of reference. It is a valuable skill to try to see things from the speaker's point of view, rather than our own. We are all different. We come from different backgrounds, have different cultures and different experiences, and it is no wonder that we see things differently. Rather than telling the speaker that you don't see it that way, say "Wow, do you see it that way. That's interesting."

5. Use positive body language

When you are listening, make sure you get eye contact, lean forward, smile, nod and use your other body language skills to show that you are listening, intently.

How do I get the other person to listen to my point of view?

When there's a difference of opinion, how do I get the other person to listen to my point of view? This is a difficult question. Even though you have applied rules 1 to 7 (above), people sometimes just refuse to listen, preferring to talk, even talking over what you are trying to say.

I am sure we have all had this experience. You are telling your friend about an experience you had last week, in the centre of town. Before you get half way through, your friend is trying to interrupt to tell of his similar, only a little bit more dramatic, experience. But it doesn't stop there. As your friend starts to tell you his tale, only half of your mind is listening. The other half is thinking about what you want to say next and before he finishes, you are leaning forward, struggling to contain your even more dramatic experience. And so it goes on..

I occasionally get asked to consult with companies about the communication problems throughout their organisation.

I would start by talking to the people on the ground. The people who do the work. Invariably, after I have achieved a level of trust, they all have an opinion about how things could be improved. Most often, at the end of the conversation, I hear the lament "But we've told the boss this but nobody ever listens."

Then, I go to management and they say "We've told the guys on the ground what to do but you can talk 'til you're blue in the face, they never listen."

Then of course there is the vast array of middle management, all focused on one department or another. In some companies, the interdepartmental discussions feel like a battle ground, but when asked they all have an opinion about how the problem can be fixed.

Sales "I've told the guys in admin how the problem can be solved but nobody ever listens."

Production "We've just come from an hour long discussion with Transport, but we might as well have been talking to that wall over there. We solved their problems for them but nobody ever listens."

Human Resources "After four days negotiating with the union, we might as well have been talking to ourselves, nobody ever listens"

Of all the problems, one sees in large and small organisations, this is the most common and surprisingly easy to fix.

When you are having a difference of opinion, you instinctively want to get your message across, so does the person with whom you are arguing. You do not want to listen to his point of view. Why should you when you know you are right? The problem is, he feels the same way and stalemate often occurs. In order to get people to listen to us, we think we have to:

Speak first - speak loudest - and speak longest

I would like to share with you an incident that happened to me, a few years ago. I have 5 children and this story is about two of them. Keswyn-Lacey, she was 8 at the time of the story and Michaela-Pascal, she was 2.

Keswyn-Lacey had been given a new juice bottle to take to school with her lunch but this was not just any ordinary juice bottle. This was a special juice bottle. Nobody else in the school had a juice bottle like this, and Keswyn-Lacey was the envy of her friends. Everybody wanted to try it. When she came home, she was full of excitement and told us of the new friends she had made.

She was so excited that we let her have the juice bottle at the table during dinner but after dinner, the bottle was forgotten as the evening routine took over. (Enter the two year old)

Michaela-Pascal had been quiet during dinner but when we had finished, she wanted to know what all the fuss had been about. Finally, she managed to get into the dining room on her own and taking the juice bottle from the table, she sat in the corner and proceeded to chew a hole in the bottom.

Nobody knew she was there of course, until we heard the cries of a two year old getting soaked with juice from the hole she had just made. The worst was yet to come. When Keswyn-Lacey discovered what had happened to her pride and joy, the bottom fell out of her world. Like unexpected thunder, she burst into howls of uncontrollable crying and nothing that I said would placate her.

Me "Don't worry darling, it's not important, it's just a juice bottle"

K-L "It's not just a juice bottle, sob... sob... sob ... it's a special juice bottle. Howl ... Nobody has ever had a juice bottle cry... cry... like that juice bottle."

Me "Not to worry darling, we can get another one"

K-L "We can't get another one, not like that one, and I promised my special friend that she could use the juice bottle tomorrow. I can't go to school tomorrow, I can't go to school ever again, howl ..... howl ....howl ..."

Anyway, this went on for a while and I had no idea what to do. The more I said that it wasn't important and that she shouldn't be silly, the more she said that it was important and we were spiralling downwards. I felt that I had to do something, so I tried to change my approach completely.

Me "No, you're right ... it is important, I can see that now.... I was wrong."

Almost instantly, the sobs came to an end. Then she said,

K-L "Well ... maybe we can get another tomorrow before school, well ... not before school but after school .... or on Saturday, maybe."

I thought long and hard after this session because I wasn't sure what had happened.

About six months later, I was dabbling on the outskirts of NLP (Neuro-Linguistic Programming) and I came across the answer. They have a word for what I experienced. They call it "Pacing."

They say (and I fully agree) that if you want somebody to listen to your point of view, you must first make sure that you have listened to and demonstrated your understanding of, their point of view.

Pacing is the process of mentally walking side by side with the person you want to influence. Not in front leading them, nor behind pushing them. Beside them, listening until they believe you fully understand. That doesn't mean that you have to agree. Simply that you have done all you can to see the problem from their point of view. Pacing is more than just listening empathetically; it is also using all the

communication tools at your disposal, to let the person know that you are with them all the way.
Once you have demonstrated that you understand, they are far more likely to listen to what you have to say, and in that way, come to a conclusion that you can both accept.

Pacing is a wonderful tool to use in communication. When you have a difficult customer, you can take the sting out of the complaint by pacing them. When you have an angry member of staff in the office, pace them and the anger subsides.

When the union are threatening to strike, pace them. Make sure that they know you are fully understanding of their point of view, and they are much more likely to listen to your point of view.

When the transport department refuses to listen to what you have to say, pace them. Listen to their point of view first, becoming fully aware of their situation before you try to tell them yours. When it comes to your turn, they are much more likely to listen sympathetically.

Pacing has one other major advantage in all communication. Once you are fully aware of their point of view, you are in a much better position to construct your argument in a way that they will accept.

Speak last - speak shortest - and speak softest

Communicating with the Opposite Sex

Look at these two pictures and tell me what you notice about them. Take your time now, we don't want to make a mistake. Okay, write down what you notice about the two pictures.

So what do you see? No, it's more obvious than that!

They're different!

Men and Women are different. This is not a revelation. Most people would say they know that. They know that men and women are different. So, if they know, how come, soon after the honeymoon is over, they expect each other to react in the same way?

Communication between many married couples begins to deteriorate after a few years and often, never picks up again. How often have you heard some of the following comments?

John "I don't understand Mary. She talks about her problems, but when I tell her how to fix them, she gets angry."

Sue "I don't think Bill loves me any longer. I know he's got a problem at work but he won't share it with me."

George "You know, Jean keeps trying to change me. Hell, if she wasn't happy with the way I was, why did she marry me?"

Shirley "I can't even make suggestions to Fred any longer without him biting my head off."

Any of these sound familiar?

When communicating with your partner, the rules we have already discussed, still apply. The first two rules, however, are the most important.

Rule 1 The success of the communication is still the responsibility of the communicator. That's you! There is absolutely no point in resorting to "What's the matter, you got cotton wool in your ears? Here, watch my lips!"

If your partner does not fully understand and accept what you are trying to communicate, then it's your fault, not his or hers. If you find yourself in this situation, read to the end of this chapter and then go back to the beginning of the book and start again. All the rules apply and, if applied, will work!

Rule 2 The focus of any communication should be on the audience (or in this case your partner). You have to start by accepting that men and women are different. They think differently, they react differently, they handle problems differently, and they naturally like to do different things.

Once you accept this and accept that in order to communicate successfully, you have to understand the needs of your audience (your partner). The next stage is to ask "How are they different?"

"Ah, well I am glad you asked"

Now this is meant to be a book on communication, not a comparative study of human psychology. However having raised the issue and, as poor communication between the sexes is probably the single most important factor in relationship breakdowns, I will contribute the next few pages to a brief summary of the most important communication differences between men and women.

Managing Problems

Men.. When a man is faced with a problem, he likes to find a place on his own and solve it. He will mull it over in his mind until he has a solution, then he is happy.

Women. When a woman has a problem, she likes to talk about it. She likes to get it out in the open, to exercise it. Once she has done that, she feels much better. She may not have a solution yet but just talking about it, seems to make it easier to manage.

Arriving home from work

Men : When a man comes home from work, he likes to unwind before he talks to the family. He may read the paper, or watch the news. This is his way of changing the activity in his brain from the "work mode" to "family mode". Ideally, he would like to get away on his own for a while but that is often not possible, so he buries his head in the paper.

Women: When a woman gets home from work, she likes to talk about her day, to tell her partner the difficulties she has faced and what the new girl is like. She needs this time to chat, in order that she unwinds successfully. She does not want advice at this stage, however, just to talk about the day.

In the home

Men: Men see their responsibility in the home as the fixer. It is the man's job, he thinks, to get things done, to fix the broken. (Be it a tap washer or a broken heart.) A man will want to make it work again, in the quickest possible time.

Woman: Women, on the other hand, see themselves as improvers. When they can see a way to improve the home, they will go for it. (That's why we all have a cupboard in the kitchen stuffed with extremely useful, but unused Tupperware). This desire to improve, does not stop with inanimate objects, however. If they find a way to improve their husband or children, they will go for that with the same vigour as reorganising the lounge.

Ego

Men: Men have a huge ego that is easily dented. Men see themselves as the "protector" and anything that damages that image, hits hard on the ego.

Women: Women have a more manageable ego that is far more stable. They are quite happy to see themselves as the "protected" but are not sure what all the fuss is about.

I am sure you are able to relate to most, if not all of the above. The major problems start to arise when you mix up the situations and the way in which the sexes instinctively react.

Let's have a look at the statements with which we started this section and see how they may arise and how they could be better handled.

John "I don't understand Mary. She talks about her problems, but when I tell her how to fix them, she gets angry."

Mary comes home late from work. She is tired after another difficult day. When she sits down John gives her a drink and says

John "You look beat, had a tough day?

Mary "Yes, it's the boss. He never gives me a minute's peace. I've got this report to finish but now he's asked me to help with the open day on Friday."

John "That's not fair."

Mary "And, he knows I was hoping to get Friday afternoon off, to see Gran in Hospital."

John "Why don't you tell him?"

Mary "No, I can't, he's got his own problems anyway. But I feel so guilty about Gran."

John "Well, I think you ought to tell him you've had enough of his problems and it's time for you, for a change. Tell him if he doesn't like it, he can keep his job"

Mary "Oh fine! How would we pay the school fees without my salary? I don't know why I bother telling you anything, you never listen anyway."

This is a classic tale of misunderstanding. When a woman has a problem, she likes to talk it over with a good listener. She is not looking for advice or help, she is just looking for understanding. Men on the other hand, see themselves as the fixer around the house. When there is a problem, they want to jump in with both feet and fix it. If they can't provide a solution, they will feel as if they have let their partner down in some way. Men rarely share their problems with another but when they do, it's because they're looking for advice.

Knowing this, John could take control of the communication and provide what Mary needs. A better outcome would be as follows:

John "You look beat, had a tough day?"
Mary "Yes, it's the boss. He never gives me a minute's peace. I've got this report to finish but now he's asked me to help with the open day on Friday."
John "Oh no, really?"
Mary "And he knows I was hoping to get Friday afternoon off, to see Gran in Hospital"
John "Yeah, that's right."
Mary "It's just not fair, I know he's got his own problems but I feel so guilty about Gran."
John "It's difficult, isn't it."
Mary "Perhaps I could go over and see Gran tonight and that would give me a chance to finish that report tomorrow."
John "I'll take you over, if you like and then we could pick up a take away on the way home."
Mary "You're so understanding John, that's why I love you."

****

Sue "I don't think Bill loves me any longer. I know he's got a problem at work but he won't share it with me"

Bill gets up early on Saturday morning and walks to the shop to buy a newspaper. When he arrives home, Sue is tidying the kitchen. Bill brushes past Sue and says, "Good morning," as he kisses her on the back of the head. Sue turns to say something but Bill has already gone through the lounge, into the study, where he sits and reads the paper. As the day progresses, Sue tries to interest Bill in a day at the park or lunch at their favourite restaurant but he tells her that he has too much work to do and shuts her off completely.

Sue knows that Bill is having a difficult time at work but can't understand why he won't talk about the problem. She feels left out. After all, if she had a problem, she would want to share it with Bill. When Bill locks himself away like that, Sue feels that he may never come back and that he no longer loves her.

Sue should take control here and understand that this is simply Bill's way of handling the problem. If he needs help he will ask for it and if he doesn't ask, he thinks he's managing the problem for the moment.

Bill, on the other hand must understand how difficult it is for Sue when he shuts himself off like that. He should reassure Sue that he will not be away for ever. Something like "I'm going to be tied up most of the day but perhaps we can watch a movie together later," should do the trick.

****

George "You know, Jean keeps trying to change me. Hell, if she wasn't happy with the way I was, why did she marry me?"

Jean "You're not going to wear that tie again, are you George? You know it doesn't look good with that shirt"

George “But I like this tie!”
Jean “Yes, but not with that shirt. Why don’t you wear the one Mum bought you last year, it would certainly be better than the one you’ve got on. And have you filled in that application form yet?”
George “Oh, I don’t know if I am going to have time to study in the evenings this year. What with the new product launch in March, and three new team members to manage.”
Jean “You’re always under selling yourself, George. You’ll never get a better job if don’t study in the evenings.”
George “But I like my job, and I like this tie, and I am sick of you trying to change me.”

When a woman loves a man, she instinctively feels she should help him improve himself. Making sure that he always looks his best and encouraging him to get more qualifications, is simply an outward demonstration of the love she feels for him. Men however, see this as criticism and that dents their overdeveloped ego. While they know they are not perfect, they would prefer not to have their imperfections raised in open discussion. If they don’t make their own decisions, they feel nagged or controlled and this makes them angry.

Knowing this, should help to avoid any bitterness. Let’s try that discussion again:

George “What do you think of this tie?”
Jean “Yeah, that’s okay. ...... You know, George, your colouring has changed over the past year or so. You’re looking so distinguished now, why don’t you try that tie your Mum bought last year.”
George “The blue one?”
Jean “No the red stripe. It will make you look a million dollars with that shirt”.
George “You really think so? ... Okay”

Jean "How's the preparation for the product launch going?"
George "It's just routine now. It's hard work, but I've done it all before. And the new team members take up my time as well. I don't know why I always get the tough jobs."
Jean "Well, there's not much you could do about it is there?"
George "Well, ... If I could find time to study, I could pass those exams and get that promotion. But when have I got time to study?"
Jean "If it's that important to you, George, we could make time. I don't mind sharing you with your books in the evenings, and we don't have to watch TV."
George "Are you sure you don't mind? It will be quite a commitment for the next six months, you know."
Jean "Yes, I know, but if you want to do it, we'll do it."

****

Shirley "I can't even make suggestions to Fred any longer without him biting my head off."

Fred and Shirley are driving back from holiday and the car starts playing up. It's been a good holiday but now it is late and they have been driving for six hours, non-stop. The car is still going but missing a beat, every so often.

Shirley "What's wrong with the car, Fred?"
Fred "I don't know, I think it will be okay"
Shirley "Why don't you pull over and have a look at the distributor?"
Fred "What for?"
Shirley "You know we had problems with that before."
Fred "It'll be fine."
Shirley "I don't want to get stuck in the middle of nowhere"
Fred "We won't get stuck."
Shirley "How do you know?"

Fred   “**Look !!!** .. Leave it to me. It will be fine, go to sleep”

Of course, Murphy takes over and the car did eventually stop, in the middle of nowhere. Fred gets out, still angry and Shirley starts to say “I told you so” as Fred slams the door. Fred pushes the lead back on the distributor cap, the car starts first time and they finish the trip with no more problems.

Man sees himself as the “protector” and as such, it is his responsibility to get the woman home safely. If he needs help to do his job, especially from the woman he is trying to protect, he will feel useless. Shirley was just trying to help, but in doing so, she made Fred feel that she did not trust him to be the “protector” any longer, and this made him angry.

A better conversation would have been the following:

Shirley   “What’s wrong with the car, Fred?”
Fred   “I don’t know, I think it will be okay.”
Shirley   ”Okay darling, I’m going to sleep. Let me know if I can help.”

The outcome would have been the same, except the journey home would have been as good as the holiday.

These are, of course, selected examples. All you really need to know to communicate better with your partner, is that Men and Women are different. Don’t expect them to think in the same way, speak in the same way or react in the same way and your communication will improve dramatically.

For some, this is a problem, but not for me.

Vive la différence”

Summary

Rule 1 The responsibility to communicate well, rests with the communicator. If the communication is not working, if you are not getting through or nobody agrees with your point of view, don't blame the audience, blame yourself.

Rule 2 The focus of any communication should be on the audience. Knowing your audience, will greatly enhance your ability to convince them.

Rule 3 In advance of any communication, you should have a clear idea of your objective and your approach.

Objective
This is your destination, the reason why you are communicating and should remain your focus as you compile the communication. Avoid multiple or mixed objectives as these confuse the audience.

Approach
If your objective is the destination, then the approach is the route you take. The approach will be heavily influenced by the needs of your audience.

Rule 4 Good communication should be constructed with a beginning, middle and an end.

Beginning
In the beginning, you should get the attention of the audience and introduce them to the subject.

Middle
The middle contains the main points you wish to raise.

End
The end of your communication includes a summary of the points raised, and a close.

Rule 5 Keep it short and simple. The shorter the communication, the greater the understanding. Try to avoid long words or phrases when short ones would do. Make it as simple as possible without losing the meaning

Rule 6 Use Emotion. Buying decisions are often made emotionally. You will increase the chances of the audience buying your ideas, if you tap into their emotions.

Rule 7 Tell a story. People remember a story easier than your facts and figures.

Rule 8 Listen. The most useful communication skill is the ability to listen attentively and confirm understanding to the speaker.

Pacing
The best way to ensure that other people listen and understand your point of view is to "pace" them. Pacing is the process of listening to them first. Making sure that you fully understand what they are saying and feeling, and then

communicating that understanding with words, tone and body language.

The Opposite Sex

Fully understanding the opposite sex is certainly beyond me and most of the people I have come across in the last 40 years. There are, however, a few rules that will help in communication and anything that helps must be worth learning.

1. Men and women are different and should be treated as such.
2. When faced with problems, men like to mull them over; women like to talk about them.
3. Men like to unwind on their own, quietly; women like to talk about their day.
4. Men see themselves as the "Fixer" around the home. When they hear about a problem they want to fix it. Women like to unload their problems by talking about them.
5. Women like to improve the home and the people in it. Men have an overdeveloped ego which gets dented when somebody tries to improve them.

The Words (see page 22)
Door, Handbag, Desk, Monkey, Cigar, Apple Pie, Motorbike, Secretary, Restaurant, Elephant.

Finally

Well, there you have it. Follow these rules and your ability to communicate at all levels, will be improved dramatically. This will certainly help you earn more money, give you greater prestige and pleasure and increase your power in the work place.

Some of you may have noticed that I have left body language out of this book. This is not an oversight. As body language is a very important communication tool, there is a pocket guide dedicated to the subject and it makes no sense to repeat any of that here.

I hope you have enjoyed this walk with me through the forest of good communication skills. I look forward to working with you again on Negotiation Skills or Motivation Skills or Selling Skills or.........

Books CD's & DVD's

By Richard Mulvey

Richard Mulvey is available to speak on a variety of business and motivational subjects. His presentations are lively and entertaining leaving all the delegates with a desire to hear more and the enthusiasm to get out there and do it. These subjects are available as Training DVD's, Books, E-Books and CD's from www.amazon.com

Training DVD's **$54.95**

This series of training DVD's by Richard Mulvey are all approximately one hour long and digitally recorded in front of live audiences. The DVD's are designed to be very practical, taking the viewer through the principles of the subject in a way that is informative and very entertaining. All the DVD's are recorded live in South Africa over the last three years and are therefore up to date and relevant.

Books **$11.95**

The Business Pocket Guide series covers essential business skills in a convenient format. Each book is a 72 page, A6 size pocket book packed with information that will be invaluable in business

CD's **$13.95**

The CD's each run for about one hour and cover the same information as the Business Pocket Guide books. They are designed to be fun to listen to, and highly informative for use in the car, in the office or at home.

1. The Will to Win

There is no secret to being successful. The process has been well known and documented for many thousands of years. In this video Richard explores this process breaking it down into the following: Take control of your life; Plan what you want to achieve and focus on it; Decide to make a change and take action. The process is simple but very effective encouraging your team to set higher goals and drive themselves until they are achieved.

2. Time Management

Time is your most important resource. In this unconventional look at Time Management Richard identifies why you are bad at time management and how to get better, why some hours of the day are as much as 3 times as valuable as others, how to prioritise and make the most use of the 24 hours available to you every day.

3. You've Only Got 4 Minutes

90% of the impression you make is created in the first four minutes of meeting people. In this training program you will find 5 simple rules that will help you manage those four vital minutes and create whatever impression you want to create.

4. Handling Objections / Closing the Sale

Managing objections and the close are the most important parts of the sale but are so often handled badly. We are not good at closing the sale. In a recent study undertaken by a local security company, salespeople ask for the business in only 34% of the time and this is not unusual. In this work we make the close simple but very effective, and take the lid off all those difficult objections.

5. Better Communication

It is not what you know that matters; it is how you communicate what you know that really makes the difference. Your ability to communicate your ideas is your most important business skill, but communication is so often badly handled. Communication techniques are easy to understand and in this work we look at the basic principles and beyond to ensure your written and verbal communication is simple but effective.

6. Stress Management

8 out of 10 Executives in South Africa suffer from Stress, 7 out of the 8 deny it! In this work we look at the effects of stress in the workplace, the stress symptoms that are easily identifiable amongst your team and focus on the Stress Busters to ensure your team manages their stress reducing sickness in the workplace as well as early retirement.

7. Negotiate a Better Deal

Whether you are negotiating a multi-million rand deal or negotiating with your children to keep their room tidy, we all negotiate every day of our lives. The most modern principles for any negations are the same and in this video we look at vital techniques to help you negotiate winning deals every time.

8. Managing Meetings

Our surveys amongst South African business people indicate that we spend between 30% and 50% of our working day in meetings. Most meetings however, are about 25% effective. Meetings are a fantastic way to communicate but can also be a major waste of your time and in this work we explore ways to make your meetings shorter, and much more effective. The book and video are co-authored by Richard and Roger Knowles, a well-known attorney, speaker and meetings specialist.

9. Body Language

20,000 years ago business was a lot simpler, a man could exchange a clay pot for a leg of panther with simple nods and grunts. Business today is a lot harder but we are still using the same gestures and they remain a truer reflection of our feelings than the words we use. In this work on body language in business we explore the gestures we all use everyday and describe their meanings. We focus on how to understand your customers, how to pick out a lie, how to manage an interview or your boss and many other business situations.

10. Getting New Customers/Keeping Them Forever

If you are going to grow your business this year you will need to be more creative in the way you attract new customers. In this work we discuss the traditional methods of attracting new customers and explore some more creative ways to dramatically grow your business. In this work we also explore simple but effective ways to hang on to your customers and keep them coming back over and over again.

11. Selling Quality at our Higher Price

It is easier to sell the higher priced product but few sales people understand this principle. Price is not the only issue as far as your customers are concerned, value is what matters and in this work we discuss how to get your quality message across to your customers so that you can achieve your premium price.

12. Delivering Exceptional Customer Service

Attracting your new customers is only half the battle, for your business to grow this year you need them to come back over and over again. By developing high levels of customer service you will encourage your casual customers to become regulars but having satisfied customers is just not enough and in this work Richard explores the techniques needed to generate “Raving Fans”.

13. Selling the Dream

Customers don't buy products, or even solutions, customers buy dreams. Your customers are dreaming about a better future through buying your products or Services. In this presentation Richard outlines the process of creating and selling the dream that the customer wants to buy

14. Selling Over the Telephone

We all use the telephone but how many of us learn to use it efficiently? In this work Richard describes the principles involved in selling your product or service over the telephone, as well as a useful script for making an appointment, techniques to get past the "Gatekeeper", and other ways to use the telephone to help you to close more sales and grow your customer base.

15. Presenting for Profit

Presenting your ideas or products to audiences large or small is something we all have to do from time to time, but statistics show that most of us hate it! This work will help you develop your presentation skills and reduce stage fright to a minimum.

16. Selling Face to Face

Selling is all about understanding your customer's problem and providing just the right solution. It is no longer enough to simply uncover customer's needs however; you have to go beyond Need to Wants and finally Desires if you are going to beat your competitors to the finishing post. In this work we look at the process that happens from start to finish in a customer meeting. Creating the right impression, uncovering his needs and the emotional reasons he will buy, right through to the close.

17. Change Management

Change is one of the most fundamental influences of modern business. You either adapt or die! In this work Richard explores the pitfalls and provides some solutions that will help your team keep up, and adjust to their ever-changing circumstances.

18. Memory Management

It is said that we all have a photographic memory; only some of us forget to put the film in. This old joke has a surprising amount of truth and in this work Richard will take you through the process of discovering your ability to use your own, very powerful memory. With a few very simple techniques by the end of the work you will easily improve your ability to remember almost anything.

19. Achieving Peak Performance

Has your team performed well this year? Think what you could achieve if they are all performing at their peak every day. We all know it's attitude that makes the difference and in this work Richard demonstrates how to develop and maintain a winning attitude.

20. Decisions

We are faced with many decisions. Should we expand? How far should we push the budget? How am I going to sell more this year? But how do you make sure you are making the right decision? In this work Richard will outline the logical approach to making accurate decisions and show how to make decisions stick.

Perception Business Skills
P O Box 201622 Durban North 4016 South Africa
Phone: +27 31 5635316 Fax: +27 31 5635432
info@richardmulvey.com www.richardmulvey.com

CPSIA information can be obtained
at www.ICGtesting.com
Printed in the USA
LVOW04s1324301215
468454LV00028B/667/P

9 781919 951775